EMBRACE THE GOD

He is the Lord of the Wild, the Great Father, the Divine Son, the Beloved Consort . . . the God is the masculine principle of the universe. In order to seek and find the balance in our lives, we must first find it in the spiritual. The balance exists with the Goddess and the God—both are necessary, for with the balance created by their cosmic union comes wholeness and holiness.

Book of Hours: Prayers to the God is a companion to *Book of Hours: Prayers to the Goddess.* The two can be used together, or this book can stand alone if you prefer to focus on the God in your devotional practice. It is ideal for solitary practitioners who prefer the ritual of structured prayer, or for use in group prayers or rituals.

Inside you will find prayers to celebrate the many faces of the God. This collection includes daily prayers and prayers for the Wiccan holy days, as well as those that celebrate the God as Sun and Moon, with special sections addressing the particular experiences and needs of men and women. Completing this collection are prayers for daily and special occasions. Embrace the god and open your heart to the fire of the universe.

ABOUT THE AUTHOR

Galen Gillotte has been a Solitary Wiccan for more than twenty years. She believes that it is important to honor her hermit self, and seeks silence, solitude, simplicity, and prayer as a way to follow the Goddess and the God, and to maintain balance in her hectic life.

She enjoys writing, reading fantasy and horror novels, creating original needlepoint art, playing the bowed psaltery, and collecting thimbles. Pre-Raphaelite art, Celtic music, and the smell of fresh herbs feed her soul. Galen lives in southern California with her dog, Sophie.

TO WRITE TO THE AUTHOR

If you wish to contact the author or would like more information about this book, please write to the author in care of Llewellyn Worldwide and we will forward your request. Both the author and publisher appreciate hearing from you and learning of your enjoyment of this book and how it has helped you. Llewellyn Worldwide cannot guarantee that every letter written to the author can be answered, but all will be forwarded. Please write to:

Galen Gillotte
℅ Llewellyn Worldwide
P.O. Box 64383, Dept. 0-7387-0260-9
St. Paul, MN 55164-0383, U.S.A.

Please enclose a self-addressed stamped envelope for reply, or $1.00 to cover costs. If outside U.S.A., enclose international postal reply coupon.

Many of Llewellyn's authors have websites with additional information and resources. For more information, please visit our website at http://www.llewellyn.com.

BOOK
·OF·
HOURS

Prayers to the God

GALEN
GILLOTTE

2002
Llewellyn Publications
St. Paul, Minnesota 55164-0383, U.S.A.

FIRST EDITION
First Printing, 2002

Book design and editing by Karin Simoneau
Cover design by Lisa Novak

Library of Congress Cataloging-in-Publication Data
Gillotte, Galen, 1952–
   Book of hours : prayers to the god / Galen Gillotte.
     p. cm.
   Includes bibliographical references.
   ISBN 0-7387-0260-9
     1. Goddess religion—Prayer-books and devotions—English. 2.
   Women—Prayer-books and devotions—English. 3. Devotional
   calendars. I. Title.

BL473.5 .G535 2002
291.4'33—dc21   2002075500

Llewellyn Worldwide does not participate in, endorse, or have any authority or responsibility concerning private business transactions between our authors and the public.

    All mail addressed to the author is forwarded but the publisher cannot, unless specifically instructed by the author, give out an address or phone number.

    Any Internet references contained in this work are current at publication time, but the publisher cannot guarantee that a specific location will continue to be maintained. Please refer to the publisher's website for links to authors' websites and other sources.

Llewellyn Publications
A Division of Llewellyn Worldwide, Ltd.
P.O. Box 64383, Dept. 0-7387-0260-9
St. Paul, MN 55164-0383, USA
www.llewellyn.com

 Printed on recycled paper in Canada

DEDICATED TO THE GUYS

Clark Hood, my brother;
he has fulfilled the roles
the God has given him
with integrity, humor, and grace.

Father John Vogel,
friend and confidant,
who faithfully serves the God
within his own tradition.

Gregg E. Schneeman,
my wild Pan of the psaltery;
he woos the Goddess with music.

CONTENTS

PREFACE

Gods in captivity cater to our whims.
They are without thunder
   and fit neatly into boxes
   of silver and gold,
   or live within moldy prayers
   while we bow
   before Them and pretend
   that They exist.
We preen ourselves in unconscious
   imitation of saints kept safely at
   arm's length.
Belief is just a word and worship
   something done out of habit or the
   hope that others will judge us holy.
All the while the thunder rumbles just
   beneath our hearing,
   the flame engulfs the mountain,
   and the Spirit of the Gods, unchained,
   will sweep across the land.

ACKNOWLEDGMENTS

I want to thank Susanne Crawford, a woman of extraordinary talents, for reading parts of the manuscript and sending my thoughts down otherwise unexplored avenues.

I also want to thank Scott NiteWolf for lending his particular talents to this book. He wrote the prayers for Common of a Man's Heart. He is a spiritual teacher and writer with over twenty years of metaphysical experience. He teaches seminars, classes, private sessions, leads drumming circles, labyrinth walks, and Pagan Sabbat and Esbat celebrations. His Dharma is that of combining all truths into one eclectic and scientific practice he calls S.O.M.A. He dedicates his prayers herein to the Masculine in all, men and women alike.

I would like to thank the members of Sacred Circle for being a great support and fun group, and Persis and Chuck, owners of Kindred Spirits, for giving us a home.

And, as always, thanks to Llewellyn for finding merit with this book, with special thanks to Nancy J. Mostad, Acquisitions Goddess; Karin Simoneau, Goddess of Word and Style; and Lisa Novak, Goddess of Visual Beauty.

INTRODUCTION

*I*n the Pagan belief system the Goddess has taken ascendancy over the God. Why is this? In part it is a reaction to traditional religious systems in which many Pagans were raised. The ever-thundering and hell-fire-spewing God of the old Judeo-Christian style did not fit the reality of many people, and even the gentle Jesus did not completely resonate with some of the deeper truths that many found. Another reason is that, for many belief systems, the Deity could only be accessed by following "the rules" as devised and administered by an all-male clergy. Even today, access to the sacred remains, to a great extent, in the hands of a male elite. This same clergy sets forth rules of conduct for all their members, most especially women. These women, in turn, may have little to say in the running of their spiritual, if not their mundane, lives if they have a hope of "going to heaven" or some other desirable afterlife. A final reason that Goddess is emphasized in some Pagan beliefs is that for too long She has been suppressed, thus resulting in imbalance. Can the day exist without the night? Light without the dark? Or life without death? The Goddess and the God are two parts to a whole, and She has found Her way back into the consciousness of the planet.

From these three causes—early religious experiences, male-dominated religious systems, and the Goddess Herself seeking balance—many Pagans-to-be began seeking God on their own by exploring other belief systems. These may have involved Eastern or Native American religions, "New Age" systems, or, closer to home, different varieties of their original faith traditions. But at some point they either stumbled upon, or were introduced to, the Goddess.

And thus began a love affair with the Goddess. The world was experienced through Her triple nature of Maiden, Mother, and Crone. The rites and rituals of the Wheel of the Year unrolled in dignity and delight, and we women learned to value our femaleness and spiritual wholeness therein. If these followers were men, the sacredness of the feminine was rediscovered and recognized. All—both men and women—imaged ourselves in Her spiritual likeness. Language and symbols of the feminine were returned into the world, and everywhere women and men began to connect with one another in true equality and respect. All places became holy ground, and the transcendent was experienced in the here and now, and in every person as well as in other members of the natural world. The Goddess gifted us with wholeness, but . . .

. . . the danger exists to "throw the baby out with the bath water." In a reaction against centuries of suppression, the temptation to ignore the God in favor of the Goddess is a genuine possibility. If this is successfully accomplished, we will be right back where we started, in a state of imbalance. Again, can the night exist without the day? Dark without light? Or death without life? We need both Goddess *and* God in our prayers, rituals, worship, and consciousness to keep both inner and outer balance for the good of society, for the living planet, and for our very souls.

I have always envisioned my soul as female. She has yearned toward God—first in Her Roman Catholic incarnation, and then as a born-again Pagan. She has sought Her Beloved in the secret hours of the night and in the sere light of day, and has been enthralled by Him on more than one occasion. The very beautiful "Song of Songs" found in the Old Testament of the Christian Bible is one of the most beautiful love songs between God and His

Beloved, the soul. The tender yearning toward one another, and the eventual ravishment (meant in its meaning of "to transport with joy and delight," [*Webster's New World Dictionary*], 356) of the soul by God, is but one vision of the Sacred or Mystical Marriage that may be found at the end of contemplative prayer, or in one blinding moment of mad ecstasy.

This book recognizes the need to honor the God. It offers a collection of prayers, meditations, and affirmations for the weekdays and holy days so that you may enter into a love affair with the God, and honor and adore Him. The primary focus is to enable you to experience God as a Lover who tenderly enfolds the Beloved in His arms and in His heart.

For those who have never practiced formal prayer, a few words: In my first book, *Book of Hours: Prayers to the Goddess,* I shared some thoughts and insights on prayer in general. Some of the information bears repeating here as a grounding for your prayer experience.

WHAT IS PRAYER?

Prayer, at its deepest core, is the passionate expression of love for God. It may take the form of formal prayer, such as those prayers offered in this book, or may be a wordless and incomprehensible cry of the heart. It matters not, for God reads the intention of the soul even before it is articulated. He reaches out to answer our need in tender yearning and, if we are open to it, we may fall into His rapture, which is beyond all words, and even beyond all thought.

I plunge into
    Your rapture,
    a falling star
    dying even as I
    blaze into Your glory.
Beauty captures me in a
    net of furious light
    and I am weightless
    in arms too big for me,
    yet just the right size to bear
    me to Your heart.
The dying was but a trick;
    You never let me fall
    at all . . .

Prayer, simply put, is talking to the Deity. It is a conversation with the God in which we speak and, more importantly, keep silent. In *Book of Hours: Prayers to the Goddess* I shared four forms of prayer in which we may engage our Lover. They are the Prayer of Expectation, the Prayer of Thanksgiving, the Prayer of Celebration, and the Prayer of Contemplation.

In the first, the Prayer of Expectation, we pray to the God in the expectation that our needs will be met. The Lover will not leave the Beloved in want, and He is ever desirous to fulfill our needs. However, at times we may not recognize that a need *is* being met, especially if something "bad" seems to be happening. Rest assured that a needed lesson is being gifted to us, and that life is unfolding as it is meant to. Never lose sight of the fact that this life is but a brief moment in time before we go on to the next stage, and is full of lessons.

In the Prayer of Thanksgiving we give thanks to our Lover for His many gifts. We invite Him into our hearts and acknowledge that it is His great love for us that sustains us and brightens the very essence of our lives. Giving thanks is a natural response to His care for us—the Beloved thanking Her Lover with passionate devotion.

In the Prayer of Celebration we . . . celebrate! Alone before our altar or among friends of like mind we pull out all the stops. We sing, dance, feast, and make merry with the best of them. We celebrate our communion with our Lover who, in the guise of the mischievous Pan, enjoys a good romp! Prayer does not have to be silent and solemn all the time; we celebrate life and offer it to Him who first offered it to us.

The last prayer type is the Prayer of Contemplation. In this prayer we go apart.

We seek silence, solitude, and simplicity in order to open ourselves more fully to our Lover. We invite Him to possess us, to ravish our senses in such a way that we cease to be separate. In this way we enter into the Mystical or Sacred Marriage and, mysteriously, become one with our Lover, the God. In this ineffable place we have our home.

AIDS TO PRAYER

We may pray anytime and anywhere, but there are some things we may do that will make our prayer experiences more fruitful.

Imagine that you are in a room. All is silent. The only light comes from a pair of pure white candles placed upon a small table. Incense curls gently toward the ceiling, causing shadows to undulate around you. You breathe deeply and are transported—by the silence, by the candlelight, by the scents of cedar, of sandalwood, by the realization that a Presence is awaiting you. You raise your hands and begin to pray. . . .

Having a place that you can use just for prayer can be very helpful. It should be free from distractions and situated in a spot suited for quiet reflection. Ideally you will set up a small altar that may include images for the God and Goddess; for example, an acorn or pinecone for the God, and a sea shell or stone with a hole through it for the Goddess. You may also have statues or pictures if you wish. Symbols for the four elements—Air, Fire, Water, Earth—are always nice. These could be candles, incense, a bowl or bottle of water, and a crystal or plant. For Spirit, rose oil works nicely. You may add other things as you feel inclined. I always change my altar set-up with the changing of the seasons, but this is not necessary.

This place becomes sacred space by virtue of its use. Every time you approach your altar to pray, you are "fixing," in your heart and unconscious mind, that this is where you will meet God. With repetition your prayer experiences will become more grounded in your psyche, and eventually your prayer will pray itself. If this makes little sense now, with repeated practice you will see what I mean. God may be encountered anywhere and at anytime—usually at a time and place of His choosing. But by being mindful of my suggestions and by approaching prayer as a Lover receiving her Beloved, you will have a fruitful prayer life, and grow in closer union to God.

I mentioned earlier the attitudes of silence, solitude, and simplicity. Each person must explore what these mean to her or him and how best to manifest them in his or her life. Before you can hear your Lover's voice, you must be silent. Before you can meet with Him, you must be willing to go apart from others. And before you can allow Him to enter into your heart, you must empty it of distractions. Meditate on these attitudes and see how they speak to you.

Lastly, in prayer we must remember that we do not pray for negative or hurtful things to happen to others. There is an ethic in prayer that we harm none. Thus we are thoughtful about what we pray for, and eventually we find ourselves asking for less and less, while giving thanks more and more. We find that our prayer takes us into longing for communion with our Lover, where we meet with Him in the watches of the night, and are wholly satisfied.

Though I prefer to meet the God as Lover and Beloved, the God has presented Himself to us in many guises. He is the son of the Goddess, and thus may be our brother. As mothers, he may be our divine Son, as we relate to Him from the Goddess within. He is the sacrifice, the seasonally dying and resurrecting God. In some cultures He is the All-Father, thus fatherhood and all that it means may be explored. Some of his many facets include God of healing, music, fertility, the Sun, the Moon, war, communication, ecstasy, creativity, mischief, wine, sex, agriculture, magic, and death. Relate to the God in whatever way feels right and comfortable for you. Simply open yourself to Him and allow Him to lead.

HOW TO USE THIS BOOK

*I*n this book you will find prayers for each day, including an Opening (Introit) and Closing Prayer. There are also eight prayers for the holy days of the Wheel of the Year. These holy days are: Samhain, Imbolc, Beltane, and Lammas, plus the Solstices and Equinoxes. Since the God may be aligned with either the Sun or Moon, there are prayers for these facets of Him. Lastly, there are prayers for the various occasions in our lives in which we either need Him, or wish to celebrate with Him. The prayers may be prayed any time during the day or night. But if you use them in conjunction with *Book of Hours: Prayers to the Goddess,* the majority of them will better be said during the time of Afternoon Prayer (from noon to 3 P.M.), with Morning Prayer (from dawn to noon), Evening Prayer (from 3 P.M. to dusk), and Night Prayer (from dusk to dawn) being drawn from *Book of Hours: Prayers to the Goddess.*

Each day also offers a Meditation and Affirmation, but these are only suggestions—use whatever speaks to you at the moment, for this is your private time with your Lover, the God.

In any event, these prayers are yours to do with as you will. My only intent is that they will lead you into closer communion with the God. For He is the Lover who loves us enough to die for us, and to show us the way back to life by being reborn just when the days are darkest and hope is needed most. Embrace Him without fear, and allow Him to cherish you.

Part One

WEEKLY COMMON: AFTERNOON PRAYER

. . . Out of the gold air of afternoon,
One knelt before her: hair he had, or fire,
Bound back above his ears with golden wire,
Baring the eager marble of his face . . .

Rupert Brooke, "Mary and Gabriel"

1

AFTERNOON

*I*n the liquid gold of afternoon the Bright God woos the Soul. With languid grace He carries her away, His Beloved, to share illimitable joy. The Young Lord leads the dance under the unwinking eye of the Sun, as the afternoon stretches into eternity. The soul trembles on the edge of sweet surrender, embracing Love.

Lord, we come before You unafraid in the bright light of the day. We seek Your embraces, the kisses of Your mouth, the brush of fingers on fevered skin. You are the Lord of Life and greet life with feasting, and with lamentation, too, for You are also the Lord of Death. You show us the way to both live and die. Dance with us as we adventure forth and lead us to rejoicing. Teach us to always honor the truths of the heart.

INTROIT

(To be said before Afternoon Prayer)

O God of Thunder, God of Might
    set aside Your lightning bolts
    and take Your ease of love with me.
You are the God of laughter!
You are the God of all delights!
Blessed Be.

MONDAY

Lord,
O Lover of the Moon
    make love to me.
My soul burns at Your touch.
My heart opens as You seek
    my mysterious center.
All that I am I offer to You,
    Bright Lord.
You touch my dreams into being;
    You give me wings to fly
    beneath Your brilliant eye.
I pierce the shadows that hide Thee
    from me
    in one blinding moment of ecstasy.

All pain, all sorrow is forgot
   in the overpowering flood of Your love.
We will always be together—
   in truth,
    we were never apart.

MEDITATION

Who is the God to you? How have you envisioned Him and how do these visions affect how you think of yourself? Of others?

DAILY AFFIRMATION

In the Name of the God: I will see the Face of God in those I meet this day.

CLOSING PRAYER

Thanks to Thee, Lord of the Dance,
   for leading me into the deeper mysteries
   of the heart.
Be with me now and always.
Blessed Be.

TUESDAY

Lord,
Your touch is silken,
    soft like the caress of the
    Moon upon my skin.
Your desire is instinctive,
    as is my need. . . .
You stride the world in
    many guises—
    Son, Lover, Father, Sacrifice—
    Priapis in His youthful glory
    and playful arrogance;
    Zeus in His wisdom;
    Adonis, dying, blood-red
    flowers His only memory,
    crushed into Earth by dancing
    maidens' feet. . . .
Still You rise again and call
    my name—
    the urge to unite as one,
    to know,
    to need,
    is ever there.
They are holy wine within my blood;
    my soul's delight.
My elusive, hidden Lover of the night.

MEDITATION

You are the Beloved of the God. What does this mean to you?

DAILY AFFIRMATION

In the Name of the God: I will love who I am and will accept my broken places, allowing them to be filled by the God.

CLOSING PRAYER

Thanks to Thee, Lord of the Dance,
    for leading me into the deeper mysteries
    of the heart.
Be with me now and always.
Blessed Be.

WEDNESDAY

Lord,
Ancient starlight shines from
    Your eyes.
You taste like music
    and feel like the scent of

    thyme, of heliotrope,
      Sun-warmed and ripe.
My eyes cannot see You all
      at once—
      Your form shifts,
      becoming something wholly new
      and beyond my vision.
You know my name and have
      followed the thread of my being
      from life to life and
      have counted every sorrow.
You are my ancient and most constant Lover,
      the refuge of my heart.
I fold against Your strength
      as we lay among the lilies,
      a moment upon the wings of time,
      whole and complete.

MEDITATION

Meditate on the image of an acorn (a masculine symbol). What possibilities does it hold and how can you relate it to your life?

DAILY AFFIRMATION

In the Name of the God: I will embrace all possibilities and opportunities today.

CLOSING PRAYER

Thanks to Thee, Lord of the Dance,
 for leading me into the deeper mysteries
 of the heart.
Be with me now and always.
Blessed Be.

THURSDAY

Lord,
Io Pan!
Io Pan! Pan!
That ancient cry rings not
 across barren landscape;
 rather, it is sung from
 urban settings of
 concrete and glass.
The God is present
 in all our modern panoply,
 yet remains
 wild, mysterious,
 unknowable except in
 sacred ecstasy.

We think we may
    tame Him;
    in truth, His ferocious aspect
    calls us out of the safety
    of our lives,
    to dance with Him
    within a Temple solely
    of His own design. . . .

MEDITATION

God is calling your name—what is He saying to you
at this moment?

DAILY AFFIRMATION

In the Name of the God: I will embrace the Sun/Son
today and allow Him to nurture me.

CLOSING PRAYER

Thanks to Thee, Lord of the Dance,
    for leading me into the deeper mysteries
    of the heart.
Be with me now and always.
Blessed Be.

FRIDAY

Lord,
Winged heart carries
   questing feet
   ever upward to the heights.
Spirit strains along with
   eager flesh.
The still, small voice
   whispers in my mind
   and longing blossoms
   into sweet desire. . . .
Holiness pervades my
   being as darkness
   merges into light.
Spirit soars and
   flesh opens to the
   wild, sweet touch of
   the God.

MEDITATION

Desire. Passion. Longing. In what way can these lead
you to holiness?

DAILY AFFIRMATION

In the Name of the God: I will embrace desire, passion, and longing as paths to holiness today.

CLOSING PRAYER

Thanks to Thee, Lord of the Dance,
   for leading me into the deeper mysteries
   of the heart.
Be with me now and always.
Blessed Be.

SATURDAY

Lord,
The God breathes fire;
   the heavens shake with
   His power.
Awake! Awake!
Comfortable traditions
   fall beneath the
   restless thunder of His hooves.
Antlers burst into bloom
   of illuminating light,
   and the voice of the God
   booms across the land.
The gates of the sacred swing wide
   and draw me in.

MEDITATION

Imagine that you are being embraced by the God. What does it feel like?

DAILY AFFIRMATION

In the Name of the God: I will nurture someone or something in need today.

CLOSING PRAYER

Thanks to Thee, Lord of the Dance,
    for leading me into the deeper mysteries
    of the heart.
Be with me now and always.
Blessed Be.

SUNDAY

Lord,
You come in splendor
    like the Sun.
Golden. Fierce.
All-pervading.

Penetrating and enlightening
   the world.
Your eyes are a blaze
   too terrible to gaze upon,
   but Your voice is music,
   Your touch bold,
   and in dreams of wistful sleep
   You impart healing of body,
   of Spirit.
Riding Your golden chariot,
   ivory horses challenging the winds,
   You bless us;
   the radiance of Your love
   enfolds us,
   that we may be at peace.

MEDITATION

Relationships are a part of life. Pick one and think on it. How and where does the God enter in? If he doesn't enter in, why not?

DAILY AFFIRMATION

In the Name of the God: I will allow holiness to enter into all of my relationships today.

CLOSING PRAYER

Thanks to Thee, Lord of the Dance,
    for leading me into the deeper mysteries
    of the heart.
Be with me now and always.
Blessed Be.

Part Two

SEASONAL COMMON: AFTERNOON PRAYER

*But if in your thought you must measure time
into seasons, let each season encircle
all of the other seasons,
and let today embrace the past with
remembrance and the future with longing.*

Kahlil Gibran, *The Prophet*

SEASONS

The Seasons of the God are the Seasons of His living and dying. He follows the Wheel of the Year unhesitatingly and teaches us how to live. At the Winter Solstice He is born, a small candle against the dark, but mighty and tenacious. He grows to manhood, sharing the dance with His Beloved, the Goddess in every woman, until His seed is sown—the fruits of love, of labor, of creativity. Then He embraces death and enters once again into the World Womb, gestating in silence, only to be born again. The Seasons of the God are the Seasons of our living and dying, and the rebirth of Spirit into flesh once again.

Lord, we ask Your blessing upon our dance. Grant that we may imitate Your love of the dance and of the Goddess. By embracing both we may live life to the fullest. You are the Master of our steps as You partner us, and the Goddess, through the Year. Lead us well through the forest of dreams, into realities yet unforeseen.

INTROIT
(To be said before Afternoon Prayer)

O God of Thunder, God of Might,
   set aside Your lightning bolts
   and take Your ease of Love with me.
You are the God of laughter!
You are the God of all delights!
Blessed Be.

SAMHAIN
(October 31)

Lord,
The solitary motion of
   the heart
   can be found on the edge of
   Winter's shadow.
The Great God sleeps.
The Mother's womb grows
   every sort of possibility
   and holds the kernel of returning light.
The absence of the God
   provides opportunities for
   inner seeing;
   visions unfold like the
   unveiling of the Sun
   from morning mist.

I seek the God in
   hidden landscapes of my
   silent soul as
   He sleeps and dreams
   me into being.
The Dark Night cloaks
   revelation in the
   God's enigmatic heart.

MEDITATION

What kernels of possibility are hidden in your heart
awaiting revelation?

DAILY AFFIRMATION

In the Name of the God: I will honor my visions,
and dream dreams.

CLOSING PRAYER

Thanks to Thee, Lord of the Dance,
   for leading me into the deeper mysteries
   of the heart.
Be with me now and always.
Blessed Be.

YULE

(Winter Solstice, December 21)

Lord,
The Dark Night
   gives way.
The God is born this day.

The sacred silence of Winter
   slides into the light—
   no longer shall we be ruled
   by the night.

The Dark Night
   gives way.
The God is born this day.

The day dawns with bright promise—
   shadows are undone.
Chains of darkness are shattered
   by the Sun.

The Dark Night
   gives way.
The God is born this day.

Rejoice in the coming of the light!

MEDITATION

What does the returning of the Sun/Son mean to
you? What connotations does "light" have for you?

DAILY AFFIRMATION

In the Name of the God: I will revel in the light, in
all its permutations.

CLOSING PRAYER

Thanks to Thee, Lord of the Dance,
    for leading me into the deeper mysteries
    of the heart.
Be with me now and always.
Blessed Be.

IMBOLC
(February 2)

Lord,
The young Lord bursts
    forth in joyous strength.
The Maiden dances
    coyly away from Him,
    seeking the shape of the doe.
The virile stag keeps pace with Her
    as She becomes the wild dove
    and He the stooping hawk.

She plummets into the raging stream,
    fighting the rapids and rising
    in rainbow splendor,
    the God a burst of light
    in Her wake.
They arise—jeweled dragons
    in flight,
    illuminated by the Sun.
The courting dance begins anew.

MEDITATION

How is the courting dance between you and your
Beloved unfolding? What transformations have you
experienced from realizing that He loves you?

DAILY AFFIRMATION

In the Name of the God: I will accept the God's love
in my life today.

CLOSING PRAYER

Thanks to Thee, Lord of the Dance,
    for leading me into the deeper mysteries
    of the heart.
Be with me now and always.
Blessed Be.

OSTARA

(Spring Equinox, March 21)

Lord,
The Moon and Sun meet
   in perfect harmony.
Day and night are set apart;
   two halves of creation
   juxtaposed,
   awaiting the symmetry of
   God and Goddess
   as They dance the
   strengthening of the light.
Life surges beneath Their feet;
   the cycle unfolds as the
   laughter of Gods
   ring in the Spring.

MEDITATION

Equal day and equal night—where do you need more balance in your life?

AFFIRMATION

In the Name of the God: I will conduct a spring cleaning of heart, mind, and spirit, that I may allow the new life and energy of Spring to enter into in my life.

CLOSING PRAYER

Thanks to Thee, Lord of the Dance,
    for leading me into the deeper mysteries
    of the heart.
Be with me now and always.
Blessed Be.

BELTANE
(May 1)

Lord,
The fiery God emerges from
    night's embrace.
He stalks the bright object of His desire
    with passionate determination and
    needful longing.
His Lady dances garbed in
    Summer's dazzling chaos.
She beckons with the slanting
    smile in Her eyes,
    the seduction of Her hips and
    breasts heavy with promised delight.
Her scent fills His senses
    beyond all thought as
    He reaches out to capture Her.

Summer's brilliant splendor blooms
   in His arms.

MEDITATION

How is sex holy? Do you have any attitudes that affect
your thinking and feelings about this?

DAILY AFFIRMATION

In the Name of the God: I will be aware of my sexu-
ality and embrace it today.

CLOSING PRAYER

Thanks to Thee, Lord of the Dance,
   for leading me into the deeper mysteries
   of the heart.
Be with me now and always.
Blessed Be.

MIDSUMMER

(Summer Solstice, June 21)

Lord,
As days lengthen
   in Summer's embrace
   the Maiden becomes the Mother.
The Oak Lord
   strides the forest
   in antlered glory,
   seeking His willing Consort.
Riotous bonfires spark
   merry revelry;
   the night draws forth
   the Sacred Dance,
   while the Lord becomes again the
   Hunter of the Moon.

MEDITATION

Roles change with the changing seasons of our lives.
Think about the many roles you play or have played.
What emerges for you?

DAILY AFFIRMATION

In the Name of the God: I will be mindful of the
roles I play and invite the God's help in those I strug-
gle with.

CLOSING PRAYER

Thanks to Thee, Lord of the Dance,
    for leading me into the deeper mysteries
    of the heart.
Be with me now and always.
Blessed Be.

LAMMAS
(August 2)

Lord,
The death of Summer
    draws near—
    the dying God hangs
    upon the air.
In sacrifice will others live;
    a lesson in love.
But also comes the knowledge that
    death is but the dream
    from which we wake.
The God is our vision
    of rebirth,
    a surety that death is but
    a moment spent in the womb of time
    with countless lives to live
    arrayed before us.

Death hangs upon the air—
    the gateway of Tomorrow awaits.

MEDITATION

What is the nature of sacrifice? What images of death
do you hold?

DAILY AFFIRMATION

In the Name of the God: I will be aware of the life
dying around me today and of how all things return
unto the God.

CLOSING PRAYER

Thanks to Thee, Lord of the Dance,
    for leading me into the deeper mysteries
    of the heart.
Be with me now and always.
Blessed Be.

MABON

(Autumn Equinox, September 21)

Lord,
The Lord has gone to sleep
   while Maidens' weep.
The edge of death
   conceals the ivory bones
   of Winter from our sight,
   as equal day and equal night
   gives way to the dark.
The silence in our hearts
   proclaims the end of Summer
   and the passing of the light.
The sorrowful Maidens' weep,
   for Winter keeps
   all things to Herself.
The dormant God gestates
   within the womb of Fate,
   and dreams He is the coming
   of the light.

MEDITATION

Equal day and equal night. Where do you need more
balance in your life?

AFFIRMATION

In the name of the God: I will seek balance in thought, word, and deed today, in order to be open to the God's visions.

CLOSING PRAYER

Thanks to Thee, Lord of the Dance,
    for leading me into the deeper mysteries
    of the heart.
Be with me now and always.
Blessed Be.

Part Three

COMMON OF THE MOON

Riding the Chariot of Night,
a diadem of stars upon His brow,
the gentle God casts His silvery light—
while blessings from His heart He does endow.

Galen Gillotte

THE MOON

All cultures have myths and stories about the Moon. Most recognize a Moon Goddess. However, some cultures reverse this and ascribe the Sun to a Goddess and the Moon to a God; for example, the Japanese Sun Goddess Amaterasu and the Moon God Tsukiyomi. Because of the cyclic nature of the Moon, the God may be envisioned as the Young Lord, the mature God at the height of His powers, and the Dead God, who takes His rest prior to becoming born again. He may be seen sailing the night skies in His chariot of silver pulled by milk-white steeds of star dust. He is the embodiment of magic. The New Moon is a time of new beginnings while the Full Moon is the fulfillment of our hopes and dreams and magical workings. The Waxing Moon is a time for drawing those things we desire to us, while the Waning Moon is for release. The Dark of the Moon, just before the New Moon, is a time of rest. So when you need to be reassured of the God's presence, look to the sky.

INTROIT

(To be said before Afternoon Prayer)

O God of Thunder, God of Might,
    set aside Your lightning bolts
    and take Your ease of Love with me.
You are the God of laughter!
You are the God of all delights!
Blessed Be.

NEW MOON

(Afternoon Prayer)

New Moon rising,
    but a hint of promise
    in the darkling sky.
The Lord releases but a
    fraction of His light
    as token of His presence.
We hang our hopes upon
    His silvered horns
    and dream of new beginnings.

MEDITATION

New Moon is a time to initiate change. What change
do you need in your life right now?

DAILY AFFIRMATION

In the Name of the God: I will begin the steps to
initiate a much needed change in my life.

CLOSING PRAYER

Thanks to Thee, Lord of the Dance,
    for leading me into the deeper mysteries
    of the heart.
Be with me now and always.
Blessed Be.

FULL MOON
(Afternoon Prayer)

The chariot of the Moon
    awaits the coming of the night,
    its milk-white horses glowing
    and eager for the flight.
The silence of the dark has
    swallowed up the day;
    the Lord now has the night
    completely in His sway—
    and as He treks across dark skies
    He scatters His bright seed,
    'till with the promise of the dawn
    He graciously recedes.

MEDITATION

What does the Moon God mean to you? How does He move you?

DAILY AFFIRMATION

In the Name of the God: I will reflect the Moon God's light in all I do today.

CLOSING PRAYER

Thanks to Thee, Lord of the Dance,
    for leading me into the deeper mysteries
    of the heart.
Be with me now and always.
Blessed Be.

Part Four

COMMON OF THE SUN

Great, glowing Disk,
O Golden One.
With voices raised
we praise
the God of the Sun.

Galen Gillotte

THE SUN

The positive attributes of the Sun include focused activity, the power of the will, passion, inspiration, intellectual acuity, determination, perseverance, integrity, healing, growth, spirituality, clarity, truth, and open-heartedness. The Sun God may be fierce in His demands upon us to pursue, attain, and maintain them. There is no place for shadows in our lives when we pay homage to the Sun. He will mentor us at need, but we must be willing to follow Him without question. Though His demands may be unstinting, He is also there to be our guard and our protector. As He tracks the skies by day, give thanks for the warmth, energy, and life that He gives by the shedding of His light.

INTROIT

(To be said before the following prayers)

O God of Thunder, God of Might,
    set aside Your lightning bolts
    and take Your ease of love with me.
You are the God of laughter!
You are the God of all delights!
Blessed Be.

MORNING SUN

The morning Sun gently
    gilds the dawn;
    each drop of dew
    becomes a glistening jewel.
The Lord awakens from sleep
    to touch our souls,
    and flings Himself into
    the day's embrace.

MEDITATION

The Sun at dawn. What promise does it bring for *this* day?

DAILY AFFIRMATION

In the Name of the God: I embrace this day fully
and will live the promise.

CLOSING PRAYER

Thanks to Thee, Lord of the Dance,
 for leading me into the deeper mysteries
 of the heart.
Be with me now and always.
Blessed Be.

SUN AT ZENITH

Fierce, fiery,
 unremittingly bright,
 the Lord demands
 homage and sacrifice.
He chases all the shadows
 of our souls away,
 revealing realities both harsh
 and bold.

To embrace Him is to
     become the flame;
     to release the outer shells
     we hide behind and
     become bold warriors
     of the Sun.

MEDITATION

There are no shadows where you are. What does the
light reveal?

DAILY AFFIRMATION

In the Name of the God: I will find my Truth and
live it.

CLOSING PRAYER

Thanks to Thee, Lord of the Dance,
     for leading me into the deeper mysteries
     of the heart.
Be with me now and always.
Blessed Be.

SUNSET

The fierceness of the day
   will soon be swallowed
   by cool night.
The bright Lord of the morning
   has come to journey's end.
We give homage to the Sun
   even as He dies,
   while knowing with certainty
   that he will rise again
   upon the threshold of the dawn.
As dusk is carried deeper
   into the night,
   we bow and chant the Sun
   to sleep
   with thanks and gratitude.

MEDITATION

Another day is done. What was good about it? What do you wish you had done differently?

DAILY AFFIRMATION

In the Name of the God: I accept the light and dark of this day with equanimity.

CLOSING PRAYER

Thanks to Thee, Lord of the Dance,
    for leading me deeper into the mysteries
    of the heart.
Be with me now and always.
Blessed Be.

Part Five

COMMON OF A
MAN'S HEART

He emerges from the shadows,
his eyes full of light
and mystery,
and holds out to me
his heart in trembling hands.

Galen Gillotte

A MAN'S HEART

Men are holders and participants in the Mystery. Because our society disapproves of a man revealing his feelings or his fears, or even his hopes and dreams, men tend to hide these gems of themselves away from the light. Sometimes they may open up to someone they love and share these hidden parts of their souls, but it takes a lot of trust on their part to do so. Scott NiteWolf has dared to disclose some of the hidden places of his heart in order to allow you into the Mystery that is him. In doing so he has shared various roles he has found meaningful in his life. It is hoped that these prayers, written by a man for other men, may help others to tap into their own Mystery and to dare to reveal their visions.

INTROIT

(To be said before the following prayers)

The man I am do you truly see
    or just the things you make of me.
I cry within but show anger without.
I long for love but rather shout.
My pride is sure but I hide my doubt.
The man I am do you truly see
    or just the things you make of me.
I need your help but alone I stand,
      your Provider, Defender was not my plan;
      I'm gentle and kind, please take my hand.

POET

Unto the worlds of words I speak.
To all who hear and beauty seek.

Those visions deep which eyes don't see.
My heart, my soul, my thoughts set free.

Phrase by phrase and word by word.
Revealed to you in sweet accord.

So frail and few those words I find.
That reach within, transcend the mind.

Wondrous lands and dreams galore.
We share these moments, wanting more.

Unto the worlds of words I speak.
To all who hear and beauty seek.

MEDITATION

Wondrous lands and dreams galore. We share these moments, wanting more.

AFFIRMATION

I am the poet, perfect and pure, whose path is clear and destiny sure.

CLOSING PRAYER: MAN

We are what we see,
   we see by what we know;
   a God a Spirit a man a boy,
   a lover a teacher with
   sadness and joy;
   a tree a rock a fiery flame,
   always strong in fear or peace;
   to take to give to win the game,
   we know by what we see,
   we see what we are.

LOVER

Like Sun and Moon, Earth and Sky.
Entwined forever by cosmic tie.

My pleasures rise with every glance.
Her eyes, her lips, a sweet romance.

The fire builds and burns within.
I yearn to touch her once again.

Like Sun and Moon, Earth and Sky.
Entwined forever by cosmic tie.

My passions flair without control.
Her hips, her breasts, a Lover's soul.

To know her now my only plea.
To hold, to kiss, to let love be.

MEDITATION

Like Sun and Moon, Earth and Sky. Entwined forever by cosmic tie.

AFFIRMATION

I am the Lover, perfect and pure, whose path is clear and destiny sure.

CLOSING PRAYER: MAN

We are what we see,
   we see by what we know;
   a God a Spirit a man a boy,
   a lover a teacher with
   sadness and joy;
   a tree a rock a fiery flame,
   always strong in fear or peace;
   to take to give to win the game,
   we know by what we see,
   we see what we are.

TEACHER

Take my hand and walk with me.
Take my thoughts so you can see.

I've been that way, I've walked that road.
I offer you a lighter load.

Be wise, be smart, and listen good.
You know it's right, you know you should.

I hand to you those years and years.
A wealth of wisdom of sweat and tears.

The teacher seeks a willing ear.
The student's thoughts are getting clear.

I've been that way, I've walked that road.
I offer you a lighter load.

A future great or badly planned.
The choice is yours, now take my hand.

MEDITATION

The teacher seeks a willing ear. The student's thoughts
are getting clear.

AFFIRMATION

I am the teacher, perfect and pure, whose path is
clear and destiny sure.

CLOSING PRAYER: MAN

We are what we see,
   we see by what we know;
   a God a Spirit a man a boy,
   a lover a teacher with
   sadness and joy;
   a tree a rock a fiery flame,
   always strong in fear or peace;

to take to give to win the game,
we know by what we see,
we see what we are.

HERMIT

I sit alone but not from fear.
I sit and pray; my thoughts are clear.

The crowds are close and 'round they go.
My inner thoughts they'll never know.

I see the worlds from deep within.
The good, the bad, the love, the sin.

Meditation sweet, my ohm, my breath.
To leave my shell, a hermit's death.

Enclosed by day, enlightened nights.
My cocoon transforms to higher heights.

But hide forever is not the plan.
For truth must shine to all of man.

I sit alone but not from fear.
I sit and pray; my thoughts are clear.

MEDITATION

I sit alone but not from fear. I sit and pray; my thoughts
are clear.

AFFIRMATION

I am the hermit, perfect and pure, whose path is clear
and destiny sure.

CLOSING PRAYER: MAN

We are what we see,
   we see by what we know;
   a God a Spirit a man a boy,
   a lover a teacher with
   sadness and joy;
   a tree a rock a fiery flame,
   always strong in fear or peace;
   to take to give to win the game,
   we know by what we see,
   we see what we are.

PRIEST

O great Spirit of hours and days,
    watch the children as they grow and play.
And raise them right, strong, and true,
    that one day they will follow you.

I pray each day as others ask,
    to heal, to help, a priestly task.

O God and Goddess I now do say,
    this man and woman are one this day.
And as they join may this vow last,
    two as one in ritual handfast.

I pray each day as others ask,
    to heal, to help, a priestly task.

O great Spirit of Heaven and Earth,
    please now bless this child's birth.
And give to him what's good, what's right,
    as both these parents vow this night.

I pray each day as others ask,
    to heal, to help, a priestly task.

O God and Goddess I do beseech,
    unto this frail human reach.
And heal the broken bones and flesh,
    for without your touch is certain death.

I pray each day as others ask,
   to heal, to help, a priestly task.

O great Spirit of Moon and Sun,
   bless this soul whose life is done.
And guide his Spirit through the night,
   to live again in sweet life's light.

I pray each day as others ask,
   to heal, to help, a priestly task.

MEDITATION

I pray each day as others ask, to heal, to help, a priestly task.

AFFIRMATION

I am the priest, perfect and pure, whose path is clear and destiny sure.

CLOSING PRAYER: MAN

We are what we see,
   we see by what we know;
   a God a Spirit a man a boy,
   a lover a teacher with
   sadness and joy;
   a tree a rock a fiery flame,
   always strong in fear or peace;

to take to give to win the game,
we know by what we see,
we see what we are.

MAGICIAN

Into the realms beyond flesh I go,
to bridge the gap within the soul.

Into the North, South, East, and West,
to bring back power strong and blessed.

With candle flame and cauldron fire,
I reach within and go much higher.

With herb and oil and secrets deep,
with sword and cross these words I speak.

Let power raise and swirl right 'round,
the circle's cast, the Spirits found.

By Fire, Water, Earth, and Air,
I cast my spell, my goal is clear.

The magical, mystical magician shouts,
and all the realms remove their doubts.

The good has come, the evil flees;
this spell is done, so mote it be.

MEDITATION

By Fire, Water, Earth, and Air, I cast my spell, my goal is clear.

AFFIRMATION

I am the magician, perfect and pure, whose path is clear and destiny sure.

CLOSING PRAYER: MAN

We are what we see,
 we see by what we know;
 a God a Spirit a man a boy,
 a lover a teacher with
 sadness and joy;
 a tree a rock a fiery flame,
 always strong in fear or peace;
 to take to give to win the game,
 we know by what we see,
 we see what we are.

Part Six

COMMON OF A
WOMAN'S HEART

*The God of all
embraces my heart.
He understands all of my needs
and gathers them into
a net of gold.
Once freed, they scatter,
like butterflies.*

Galen Gillotte

A WOMAN'S HEART

*W*omen are creatures of Air—we often live in thought. We plan and make lists and are eager to learn and grow. We are made of Fire, passionate with flaming tempers and equally flaming desires. We are of Water, sinking lazily into possibilities, intuiting and dreaming. Whether we admit it or not, we have visions of tomorrow; visions that embrace the limits—and surpass them. We are solid, like Earth. We persevere through hardships and we manage to manifest our needs—and the needs of those in our care—even when the odds are against us. We may have our heads in the clouds, but we stand steady on terra firma. Women are creatures of the stuff of life, and we revel in it.

The God a part of our lives, by root and branch, leaf and flower. He walks beside us; he whispers in our dreams. We turn to Him at need, or just to share our joy. Thus we invite Him into deeper communion with us.

The following prayers highlight some of those experiences in which we take His hand, finding courage, solace, or a companion with which to share. We revel in life, and dance each day with the soul-companion of our hearts.

INTROIT

(To be said before the following prayers)

Hail to Thee,
   Bright God.
A woman's heart may
   open at Your touch.
Accept these prayers,
   offered upon scented sighs.
Blessed Be.

MYSTERY

Lord,
You are the Mystery
   that fills my every breath.
You define the very
   essence of my being.

You it was Who brought
my Name into the world.
And when all is done,
You'll be the One
to gentle me through death.

MEDITATION

What is Mystery? What is the shape of His face?
The image that He has within your deepest visions?
The Mystery is all around us, within us. Let Him
embrace you now.

AFFIRMATION

In the Name of the God: I enter the Mystery by
being still and open to the prompting of my heart.

CLOSING PRAYER

Thanks to Thee, Bright God.
You take these prayers to heart
and spin them into gold
through the actions of Your love.
Blessed Be.

PASSION

Lord,
Liquid flame flows
   through my veins
   and holy wine drips from
   Your lips to mine
   as we embrace in an
   ecstasy of forgetfulness,
   and senses, abandoned,
   lead us into unhurried escape.
Heartbeats become words,
   beating with the rhythm of
   our bodies' dance,
   and speak of love,
   of passion,
   as we become one,
   dissolving into forever.

MEDITATION

Passion may be of the body, certainly, but also of the mind and spirit. What is the source of your passion?

AFFIRMATION

In the Name of the God: I am a passionate being and live my passion every day.

CLOSING PRAYER

Thanks to Thee, Bright God.
You take these prayers to heart
and spin them into gold
through the actions of Your love.
Blessed Be.

EMPTINESS

Lord,
I am empty.
I contain nothing.
The depth and breadth
of my emptiness astonishes me.
I tremble—
a single golden rose
suspended in time,
waiting to fulfill its potential.
And still I wait,
empty, silent,
a vessel aching to be filled.
Then, like a flower softly opening,
I receive You.
You overcome my senses
and flood the essential me
with Your presence.

The cup is full, content;
　　the rose a full and glorious Sun.
The God reveals Himself through me,
　　spilling outward in a wave of ecstasy.

MEDITATION

Emptiness is that state of containing nothing. It is often a time of waiting with an inner knowing that something is coming. In your emptiness, seek inward—what is it that you await? What do you need in order to be filled?

AFFIRMATION

In the Name of the God: Even in my emptiness the God is there. I let Him fill me to the brim.

CLOSING PRAYER

Thanks to Thee, Bright God.
You take these prayers to heart
　　and spin them into gold
　　through the actions of Your love.
Blessed Be.

DESPAIR

Lord,
I cry to Thee from out
   of the darkness.
My tears flow unchecked,
   falling upon barren ground.
Light and life have left me;
   the dawn will never come again.
I am bereft—
   my soul is lost to me.

In silence do You come;
   a gentle breeze the hand that
   dries my tears.
Penetrating the shadow of my Being,
   You confound me,
   drawing me into an embrace
   so all-encompassing that I gasp.
My darkness sheds from me like
   a receding sea.
Your light upholds me as
   I become the dawn.

MEDITATION

There are times that we live in the darkness of despair.
Go there now. What does it feel like? Imagine the
light of the God leading you out. What is it like to
become the dawn?

AFFIRMATION

In the Name of the God: Even in the darkness light
shines somewhere. I become that light.

CLOSING PRAYER

Thanks to Thee, Bright God.
You take these prayers to heart
    and spin them into gold
    through the actions of Your love.
Blessed Be.

INTIMACY

Lord,
You are the intimacy
    that I seek.
Divine connection
    breeds a closeness not
    merely of the body,
    but of the heart,
    the mind,
    and Spirit's breath.

Within my lover's eyes
   Divine Love looks at me,
   enfolding me in raptures
   that draw me from my Self.
Intimacy spills from an open heart.

MEDITATION

We think of intimacy as having to do with sex, but
we may engage in sex with no real intimacy. With
whom are you intimate in your life? Friends and fam-
ily? God or Goddess? The Earth? Yourself? Find the
source of your intimacy and you find hints of who
you are.

AFFIRMATION

In the Name of the God: I cast down any walls that
prevent me from experiencing intimacy in my life.

CLOSING PRAYER

Thanks to Thee, Bright God.
You take these prayers to heart
   and spin them into gold
   through the actions of Your love.
Blessed Be.

NEW BEGINNINGS

Lord,
Every day is a new beginning;
    my life
    has become a new beginning.
For better or worse,
    with joy and fear,
    the journey is begun—
    again.
It may not matter where
    or how I will end up—
    for beginnings presuppose endings.
It is the journey that is all.
And like the dragon that
    lifts upon the night sky,
    I fly alone—
    except for my Beloved,
    Who is the wind that
    carries me aloft.

MEDITATION

New beginnings can be scary. We begin a new relationship. We move into a new home. We start school, or a job, or have a child. Beginnings always seem to grow from endings of some sort. What are you currently beginning, and what has ended? Acknowledge and honor both.

AFFIRMATION

In the Name of the God: I embrace new beginnings
with eager confidence.

CLOSING PRAYER

Thanks to Thee, Bright God.
You take these prayers to heart
    and spin them into gold
    through the actions of Your love.
Blessed Be.

Part Seven

COMMON OF THE RHYTHM
OF OUR LIVES

Traveling the round of years,
joys and sorrow,
laughter, tears,
our hearts are filled with
the God's warm cheer—
just call upon His name.

Galen Gillotte

THE RHYTHM OF OUR LIVES

Our lives unfold like the lotus—beautiful, complete, and of vibrant color. We follow the round of days in the shadow of the Sun, while our nights are made of moonshine and stardust. Our hearts beat with the rhythm of the Earth, singing in concert with all Her children. And sometimes we sing of joy, while at other times sorrow is the underlying chord. Our laughter may shake the trees, or our tears find their way to the sea. In all that we do the God is present. The following prayers are for those times that we wish to honor and remember. They are for the times words desert us except for the heartfelt cry of our souls. They dance upon the tongue like spun sugar in tune with our happiness and for those special events we treasure in our hearts.

The beauty and tragedy of our stories is what makes the world ever unfolding, ever new.

Lord, we ask Your presence as we pray. By entering into our lives You make them holy. By making them holy everything we do may be a blessing. In times of sorrow and of joy we turn to You and seek your sacred light.

TO BID GREETING TO THE SUN

The night is almost done.
The Lord of the Sun
   awakens from sleep.
The peace of the dawn
   fills our souls
   at the promise of another day.
We greet the dawn
   rejoicing—
   anticipating the God's
   bright blessing upon
   this day.
Blessed Be.

TO BID THE SUN FAREWELL

The day is almost done.
The Lord of the Sun
   reaches journey's end.

A soothing peace
   infuses our souls as
   we are bathed in His afterglow.
The bright Lord has been
   our companion this day
   and now we bid Him farewell,
   holding an image of His light
   against the coming dark.
Blessed Be.

SELF-BLESSING

Upon the Winds
   I meet the God.
He blesses me with
   keen-edged thought
   and leads me to
   the Sun.

Within the Flames
   I meet the God.
He blesses me with
   passionate fire
   and leads me to
   the Sea.

Within the Waters
  I meet the God.
He blesses me with
  dream-filled visions
  and leads me to
  the Earth.

Upon the Earth
  I meet the God.
He blesses me with
  creative powers
  and leads me to
  the Spirit.

Embracing Spirit
  I meet the God.
He blesses me with
  an insightful soul
  and leads me to
  His side.

Face to face
  I meet the God.
He blesses me with
  my own Name
  and leads me to
  myself.

Blessed Be.

A WITCH'S AFFIRMATION

Lord and Lady,
In perfect love
    and perfect trust
    I shall harm none
    in thought,
    word, or deed.
I give Thee thanks
    for this most perfect day.
Blessed Be.

BLESSING BEFORE A MEAL

Lord and Lady,
I *(we)* joyfully give Thee thanks
    for the bounty set before me *(us)*.
Through the magic of
    Air and Fire,
    Water and Earth,
    may my body *(our bodies)* be sustained.
I *(we)* thank Thee for this most perfect day.
So Mote it Be.

BLESSING UPON OUR UNION

Shining Lady,
Golden Lord,
   bless our union
   now and always.
By blossom, fruit,
   and grain,
   bless our union.
By Air, Fire, Water, and Earth,
   bless our union.
Let us take our place together
   in the Sacred Dance
   with joy and gladness.
Blessed Be.

TO INVOKE PASSION

Lord,
Your bright flame
   invokes the heat—
   heat of body,
   of desire.
Fire smoldering,
   building, blazing,
   all-consuming
   inner pyre.

Falling, flying
 into bliss,
 becoming one with
 fire and flame,
 bodies, hearts, and minds
 embracing,
 till all is lost
 save for Your name.
So Mote it Be.

A CHILD'S BLESSING

By clarity of Air and
 passion of Fire—
 blessings upon this child.
By visions of Water and
 talents of Earth—
 blessings upon this child.
By Spirit's living Grace,
 Lord and Lady's bright magic—
 blessings upon this child.
May the fullness of life, laughter, and love
 be hers *(his)*.
So Mote it Be.

A BLESSING FOR OUR
ANIMAL FRIENDS

Lord of the Forest,
Lady of the Beasts,
   bless this Your creature *(name)*.
Grant that I will always
   keep faith with her *(him)*
   by providing
   love, food, and shelter
   for all of her *(his)* days.
Thank You for this most
   precious companion.
Blessed Be.

A GARDEN BLESSING

Lord and Lady,
   Earth faeries all,
   bless my garden through
   Winter, Spring,
   Summer, Fall.
Speak my flowers into bloom
   within their proper time,
   and grant that vegetables and fruits
   grow lushly in their clime.

By Air, Fire, Water, Earth,
  I give good thanks to Thee,
  that when needed most
  my garden will give peace and rest to me.
So Mote it Be.

FOR INSPIRATION

God and Goddess,
Lord and Lady,
  wellspring of all
  inspiration,
  set my soul ablaze with
  Your creative energy.
Let it manifest in
  song, or dance,
  or printed page *(include your creative endeavor)*
  for the delight of all.
Blessed Be.

FOR HEALING

God of the Sun,
Divine Physician,
   inner Healer of the Light—
   breathe Your blessing upon my
   mind and body,
   heart and soul.
Release disease wherever it's found.
As fire burns away the dross,
   so do You burn away
   any darkness that resides within.
So Mote it Be.

FOR JOY

The Dragon stirs and wakes.
Sweeping the stars with
   outstretched wings He
   trumpets the coming of the dawn.
The fading stars sing His Name
   as He flies in perfect
   concert with the Sun.
He is the embodiment of Joy.
He lifts my heart and
   sets my soul to flight
   with milky, iridescent wings.

I take that leap of faith
   and joy upholds me,
   coursing through my veins
   like holy wine,
   or like molten flames of
   morning's gold.
Blessed Be.

A PRAYER FOR PROSPERITY

Golden Lord and
Silver Lady,
   shower Your riches
   upon me.
May my life be
   full of Your prosperity
   in all its subtle hues.
May gratitude be ever
   upon my lips,
   and thankfulness in my heart.
Blessed Be.

A PRAYER FOR PROTECTION

Lord and Lady
    cast Your Circle,
    ring of fire,
    pool of light.
As I wake or
    sleep or travel,
    keep me safe
    through day and night.
So Mote it Be.

A PRAYER TO RELIEVE DEPRESSION

As the light pierces
    the darkness—
    depression, release me!
As the seedling seeks
    the Sun—
    depression, release me!
As day follows the night and
    life follows death—
    depression, release me!
By the power of the Goddess
    and the God, I bid
    thee, depart!

With the powers of
   Air, Fire, Water, and Earth,
   I greet the day, newly born.
I am free of all darkness—
   depressing thoughts fly away
   like birds.
I am myself again.
So Mote it Be.

A TIME TO MOURN

Lord and Lady,
You who gather the souls
   of the dead,
   in loving embrace,
   receive my *(friend, lover, spouse, et cetera)*
   into Your hearts and
   hold her *(him)* close.
The Wheel of the Year will
   unfold without her *(him)*;
   bless me as I carry on alone.
Merry Meet. Merry Part. Merry Meet Again.
Blessed Be.

A PRAYER FOR PEACE

Breathe in.
Breathe out.
Again . . . again.
Eyes closed,
    body calm,
    breathe in.
Breathe out.
Peace . . . I seek.
Peace . . . I find.
Peace . . . I am.
Blessed Be.

A PRAYER TO RELIEVE WORRY

Upon the Air
    my worries fly—
    away, away,
    fly now away.

Within the Fire
    my worries burn—
    to ash, to ash,
    burn now to ash.

Within the Water
    my worries sink—

to drown, to drown,
sink now and drown.

Within the Earth
my worries lie buried—
deep, so deep,
buried now so deep.

By Air and Fire,
by Water and Earth,
my worries are gone;
have transmuted to mirth.

So Mote it Be.

A PRAYER BEFORE BEGINNING
A NEW VENTURE

Blessed Lady of the Night,
Lord of the Morning Star,
as I embark upon
this new venture *(insert name, if you desire)*
grant me blessings of
completion and success.
Thank You for the talents
that will help me
reach my goal.
So Mote it Be.

Part Eight

THE FIRE OF THE GOD

Your eyes are full of flame.
Your wings drip fire.
Within Your embrace
I am drowning,
drowning
in ecstasy.

Galen Gillotte

FLAMES OF INSPIRATION

*T*he fire of the God touches my inner Self into being and I cannot help but find voice in poetry and love songs. He who ravishes my soul with delight indescribable calls forth the hidden muse so we may meet in the flames of inspiration. The following are some prayers found in the deepest silence and solitary communion with He who fills my soul with fire and sweet passion.

DANCING ON THE EDGE

It is a razor's edge,
    this thing called Love.
I dance upon it
    at my peril.
A moment's inattention
    and I shatter into a
    thousand pieces,
    never to be wholly restored
    to who I was before.

I seek the dance
    even as I fear it.

In order to dance gracefully
    I must renounce the
    safe in favor of the sacred.
I must allow my
    Beloved to lead me
    into the dangers of the
    uncharted heart.

To live without Love is
    to die in the midst of life;
    to seek Love is to risk
    the loss of the essential Self,
    or to find it.

Thus as I take that first step
    I do so with the exquisite awareness

that I will be dancing on the edge;
to plunge, perhaps, into
the Source of Love
and so find salvation within
that illimitable light.

WINGS

Before the dawn,
    still captured in the
    hush of night,
    I hear the rush of wings.
Is it just the wind
    or have You come to me?
In the darkness I wait,
    caught in the tension
    of the moment,
    between night and day;
    hope and trepidation.
I have longed for You
    for so long . . .
    gently, a feather drifts
    past my face.
I arise and take Your hand.

LIKE LIGHTNING

The God's Love strikes
　　like lightning.
My soul—
　　a flock of birds—
　　takes flight!
In startled wonder
　　I catch fire with
　　His Love,
　　blazing into
　　slivers of radiance
　　before descending
　　to Earth.
I rain down,
　　caught in the
　　whirl of Love,
　　and gently touch
　　the ground.

THE FIRE OF THE GOD

The days grow shorter,
　　colder.
The fire of the God
　　heats the hidden
　　corners of the soul.

The time for
   introspection, for
   contemplation,
   has arrived.
Not for me the fire of
   the blood,
   the passion of the flesh.
The God draws me deeper
   into the forest of my inner Self
   to seek the Source of
   all Being.
The Sun sets.
The night is full of
   errant possibilities.
I withdraw into my
   Lover's heart,
   there to await another dawn.

OFFERING

Like the fog,
   the enigmatic God
   surrounds me.
I cannot see.
I cannot speak.
I cannot hear.

Silence and solitude
  become my guides
  and lead me ever deeper
  into the essence of
  my heart.
There, without pretense,
  I offer myself up to
  the God's embrace.

SWEET DISSOLUTION

I shatter against
  the sweetness of Your love,
  shards of light
  scattering in countless
  directions.

It is too hard to be
  loved by the God, sometimes . . .

Tenderly You collect
  every piece of me
  and by some miracle
  or Art
  restore me to wholeness.

I quiver at Your touch;
    the parts of me threaten to
    fly away again like birds.

DREAMS OF THE GOD

Dreams are made of
    passion and desire,
    and images of the same
    spill into waking moments;
    we weave a tapestry of
    loving in the heart of darkness,
    for only in dreams may we meet
    and join as one.

The tapestry unravels when the
    morning Sun,
    no longer kept at bay,
    seduces me from sleep;
    yet You remain within my heart,
    my body aroused by
    the memory of Your touch
    held within my dreams.

PAN

You emerge from the
    boundary of thought,
    the scent of the Earth,
    of green, moist secrets
    clinging to Your hair;
    your body hard,
    your eyes alight with mischief.
The music You make envelopes me
    and sunders all perception
    of my Self, easing me
    down upon a bed of moss,
    of fern,
    until You hang above me and
    all my world is reflected
    in Your eyes.
I awake from the dream,
    bits of green entangled in my hair,
    the lush scent of You lingering upon the air.

AFTERWORD

*T*he God is present in the blazing Sun. He lives in the noble oak, and the storm is His voice. He is the growing grain. In prayer and meditation we meet Him in the silence and allow His love to infill us. He teaches us of fearlessness in the face of death and the knowledge of the life beyond.

This book contains a never-ending journey. The prayers within cycle around the Wheel of the Year, and though we always end up where we began, the destination holds subtle differences that generate ever-new beginnings, new avenues of thought. We are changed through the very living of these prayers and the attention we give to the unfolding of our days.

It is hoped that these daily prayers, meditations, and affirmations have helped you to grow closer to the God and to open to His abundant, wild Love. Upon distant shores or mountain peaks, within the depths of the forest or in the midst of fields of grain or upon the seemingly barren desert, He is there. But more than these, He resides within your heart and so is accessible at any time, in any place.

Falling like a star
    You catch me in Your
    net of gold.
You carry me off to
    the forest deep,
    where songs and visions
    are mine to keep.
You are the antlered stag.
You capture my heart
    as You leap away.

Bright Blessings.

Appendix

GODS

ADONIS

Greek vegetation God who dies and is reborn seasonally. He evolved from the earlier vegetation Gods Adoni, Tammuz, and Demuzi. Adonis was the lover of Aphrodite. The theme of the seasonal dying and rebirth of the God may be found in many cultures. His sacrifice represents the renewal of the land, dying so that others may live (the harvest), and the transient nature of death. In Greece, women used to plant small gardens, called "gardens of Adonis," in pots (the womb) with plants that were short-lived, thus representing the life and death cycle of the God. This ritual also gave women the opportunity to mourn and grieve for those whom they may have lost throughout the past year, and so was a form of emotional release. Adonis, like His earlier counterparts, was the son/lover of the Goddess, and the tragic love affair aspect of the myth was also played out. To experience Adonis you might want to plant a small garden in a pot for Him. Traditionally, fast-growing plants like lettuce, wheat, or millet were used. Sow the seeds in the Spring and tend the garden. While caring for it, give thought to the God who brings life to Mother Earth in His fertilizing aspect and give thanks for the food, which is His gift. When the plants have reached their peak, give the dying plants, and thus the God, back to the soil to renew it for the next planting season. Give thanks to the God for His sacrifice. Throughout this cycle one cannot help but give thought to the meaning of life and death. You may wish to mourn any lost loves, or deaths, from the past. But always know that life and love returns anew.

APOLLO

Greek and Roman God of the Sun. In His Greek aspect He was the twin brother of Artemis, who was born first and who aided Their mother, Leto, in His delivery. Apollo is also God of healing and medicine, truth, light (which is a facet of truth), magic, music, and poetry. He played the lyre, setting His poems to music. Apollo is a God of patriarchy and, as such, usurped some of the Goddesss' aspects. He was said to have killed the Python (Earth Goddess) at Delphi and took that Oracle for His own, thus becoming a God of prophecy. He also took on the attributes of the Muses and became a God of creativity and inspiration. In a sense, He becomes the God of the blinding light of inspiration and opens doors to inner transformation and healing. To get in touch with your Apollo aspect, seek the Sun. Find a garden bench and allow the Sun to wash over you. Ask this God to bless you and heal you of your hurts: "Apollo, Golden One, as You chase the wild horses of the Sun across the sky, draw from me all hurt, all illness, and with You let them fly." You may also turn to Him for creative inspiration.

CERNUNNOS

Celtic Horned God. Little is known about this God, as the Celts, not having a written language, passed along their history verbally, through bards and the Druid class. Cernunnos was a forest God, with antlers on His brow. He was flanked by wild creatures and was the Consort to the Moon Goddess. He was the Hunter of the Moon. To experience Cernunnos' wild spirit, place a crescent upon your brow and seek the wild places at the solitary hour of dawn or dusk. These are the times that creatures are stirring the most—the birds are more active then and throw their songs to the rising Sun; the bats and insects run the race of life and death at dusk. If you are by a pool or stream, you may observe various animals who come to drink. Invoke Cernunnos thus: "Cernunnos, Horned Lord, I offer myself to Thee this night *(or morn)*. Be Thou present and enfold me with Thy strength. I am the Daughter of the Moon. Be Thou the Hunter of my heart."

EROS

Greek God of erotic love. In pre-patriarchal times He was one of the first Gods to appear. In later times He was said to be the son of Aphrodite, fathered by one of the Gods, though His parentage does get a little confusing depending on your source. He married Psyche (Soul), which suggests the inter-twining of Spirit with flesh and the sacredness of such a union. His influence (Cupid's arrows) lead many into romantic, sexual love, not always with happy results! His passionate nature demands a response of complete and utter abandon. To invite Eros into your life, abandon yourself to sensuality. Take a long, hot bubble bath surrounded by candles and perfumed incense. Wear soft, silky, or slinky attire—sexy underwear beneath a proper business suit! If you have a lover, have a romantic candlelit dinner and invite him or her to participate in a night of love. If you have chosen to be solo for awhile, invite Eros into your dreams and ask Him to show you who your next lover may be.

HADES

Greek God of the Underworld and of Death, one of the major Gods of the Greek pantheon. Hades fell in love with Demeter's daughter, Persephone, in Her *Kore*—or Maiden—aspect and abducted Her. He carried Her away to His dark realm where He held Her until Demeter, refusing to allow the grain and fruits of the Earth to grow, persuaded Zeus to have Her daughter restored to Her. However, Hades encouraged Persephone to eat some pomegranate seeds (symbol of marriage, fertility, and rebirth), thereby uniting Her to Him for a season of each year. Persephone is reborn each Spring into the world; and each Autumn is reborn as Hades' Queen. Hades is a chthonic God, opening the gates of the Underworld—or the unconscious—to the seeking soul. He is not a guide; rather, He awaits the soul at the end of Her journey. There He reveals His kingdom to Her; it is Her task to discover the riches there. To experience the hidden passion of Hades, take a ripe pomegranate and retire to a room lit solely by candles. Have some music playing in the background; anything that evokes mystery and the throbbing dark. Take the pomegranate and slice it in half. Admire the deep red color and the jeweled fruit. Note how the juice drips on to your fingers. Smell the clean scent of it. Take a few of the seeds and bless them in the name of Hades. Eat and savor their tart flavor on your tongue. Close your eyes and imagine that you are in the Underworld, transported there magically by the power of the pomegranate seeds. See the splendor. Smell the rich spices and aroma of costly incense. Hear the whisper of music from the lyre, psaltery, and flute. Feel the plush carpet beneath your feet, the silks of the wall hangings. Hades is there to admit you, and He has a secret to share. Sit quietly until you uncover for yourself what it is.

LORD OF THE DANCE

This is one of the names given to the God of the Witches, for He dances the Wheel of the Year around with the Goddess. Both are needful, both are necessary to keep it turning. As Pagans, we dance with Them and rejoice in the year as it unfolds, and rejoice in our connection to our Deities, who are ever near. To connect with the Lord of the Dance, play music that really gets the blood moving. Dance, alone or with others, but *dance!* Experience the abandonment to music and movement and your own singing heart. Admire how your body moves. Know that the Lord of the Dance is with you, and open to the joy of the moment. I guarantee that you cannot come away from this ritual without feeling good!

OAK KING/HOLLY KING

Representing the waxing year and the waning year, respectively, these Gods are actually one God who shows us different aspects of Himself. He partners the Goddess throughout the Year's Wheel. The Oak King rules from mid-Winter to mid-Summer, while the Holly King rules from mid-Summer to mid-Winter. They ritually kill each other in order to claim Their crowns, but always return at the appointed time. They echo earlier rituals when the Goddess ruled and the king may only rule beside Her at Her biding and consent. Every few years or so the king must die so that a strong and fertile claimant may take his place in order to renew the land. The Oak King rules over growth and fecundity, while the Holly King rules over the time of withdrawal, contemplation, and rest from labors. To honor these Gods, at Winter Solstice you may ritually burn some holly, declaring the end of the Holly King's rule and welcoming the Oak King. At this time you may look forward to the return of Spring, of growth, of activity. You may want to write down some goals you wish to achieve in the coming months and call upon the aid of this active God. At the Summer Solstice you will burn some oak wood or leaves, bidding farewell to the Oak King and welcoming the return of the Holly King. In the midst of summer, we receive intimations of the coming Autumn, and of the Great

Silence of Winter. We harvest what we have grown, whether in our gardens or in our lives and souls, and we begin the journey inward, becoming more contemplative and inner directed as the Season unfolds. And always, the Goddess partners Him in these endeavors, as Her Consort partners us.

OSIRIS

Major Egyptian God, brother/son/lover of the premier Goddess Isis. He is both a vegetation God, dying and resurrecting seasonally, and a sacrificial God, dying and entering the Afterlife in order to save His worshippers and usher them into the bliss of eternal life. The most common story about Him has Osiris being murdered and dismembered by His envious brother Set, with Isis eventually collecting all the bits of Him and, through magic, restoring Him to life. It is noteworthy that Isis found all of Him except for His phallus, which She had to remake with magic. They then had a son, Horus the Younger, who is also mysteriously Osiris. Horus rules the living, while His "father" rules the dead. In many ways Osiris was also an archetype for the Christian God Jesus. Many of the titles adopted by the Christians for their God were said to have first belonged to Osiris: Lord of Lord, King of Kings, and the Good Shepherd. The cult of Osiris lasted for hundreds of years, and only died when it became too elaborate for the common person to follow. To have an Osiris experience, become the mourning but active Isis, seeking Her lost lover. Wear a mourning veil of black, and set black candles at the quarters of the East, South, West, and North. Place your cauldron near the candle at the West, put some potting soil in it, and plant it with any herbs or flower seeds. Water the seeds and call upon Osiris to return from the womb of death. Nurture the seeds with the coming days, and when they are big enough transplant them to your garden or to a larger pot. Every time you see them, think about how the God of life may renew your life again and again.

PAN

Originally a God of Arcadia in the Peloponnese, He eventually became one of the major Gods of Greece. He has the lower body of a goat, and goat horns upon His head. In time He became associated with the witches' Horned God, who degenerated into the Christian concept and image of Satan. "Pan" means "all" in Greek, and though He is known as the God of the forest and wild creatures, all of nature is His realm, even the local city park or one's own backyard. Pan is a lusty God and had many affairs. The words "panic" and "pandemonium" come from His name, which may be a clue to Pan's "playful" side. But beware—do not anger Him or panic and pandemonium may follow! Pan does enjoy a good time and has been associated with Dionysus, God of wine. He is also a God of music; He created and plays the panpipes (one myth has Him pursuing a nymph by the name of Syrinx who, in order to escape, was turned into a reed by her father. Pan then cut down the reeds and made pipes, which He played), and His music is haunting and evocative of His presence. Pan is unself-conscious in His living and loving. He is supremely confident in everything He does and He has the gift of living in the moment. To invoke these aspects of Pan for yourself, go to any natural spot—the forest, the beach, or your own backyard. Take with you a musical instrument of some sort—if you don't think you can play one, think again! A drum, tambourine, maracas, even a set of wind chimes can be used. Find a comfortable spot to sit. Softly and gently begin to play random notes (drumbeats, et cetera) on your instrument. Chant along with the beat (silently if you're playing a woodwind): "Io Pan! Io Pan! Io Pan, Pan!" When you feel the presence of the God—stop. Meditate upon those qualities you want this God to help you incorporate into yourself—confidence, the ability to play, have fun, and live in the moment, wholehearted surrender to physical enjoyment, the connection to the natural world, or a wicked sense of humor, for example. Then go forth, and when you feel yourself in a situation in which one of these qualities would be appropriate, think of Pan and let Him be your guide.

PRIAPUS

Early fertility God of Asia Minor, eventually becoming a God of the phallus, usually portrayed with enormous genitals or simply as a huge penis. Though this may seem shocking to us moderns, when one thinks about it our own culture tends to almost worship sex and place great importance on how well one is endowed. To invoke Priapus in His context of fertility God, engage in any activity that may result in growth and creativity, whether it be making love for the purpose of creating a child, planting a garden, or engaging in a creative pursuit that will result in the "growing" of a painting, a story or book, or the transformation of flour and other ingredients into homemade bread. Call upon Priapus to "fertilize" your activity, and give thanks to this ancient God of creation.

ZEUS

The supreme Father-God of the Greeks, often portrayed as contentious, demanding, vengeful, unfaithful to His wife Hera (and His earlier spouses), and deadly to His children. The pre-classical Greek form of Zeus portrayed Him as one of the seasonally dying Gods, a fertility God, a virgin-born God, and subject to His Goddess-mother. Eventually He took over Mt. Olympus and became the patriarchal king of all the Gods, who were jealous of His position and His power. One of the symbols of Zeus was His thunderbolts, which could be loosed on His enemies without warning. However, He was also at times kind and loving to some of His children, granting Artemis' wish to be virgin (Her own woman). So He was not all bad. But what to say about Zeus and His place in our lives? On the face of it He is not a very desirable God to get to know! However, we *can* learn from His domineering, patriarchal example: He may stand as a warning to us to never allow this form of energy to take dominion again. Spend some time in quiet meditation to determine if this negative energy exists in any way, shape, or form in your life. If it does—a battering spouse or lover, an untenable work situation, being abused or minimized in any way— imagine yourself with one of Zeus's thunderbolts and loose it at whatever or whomever is causing damage in your life. Then, if needed, seek out a counselor, shelter, or other positive assistance to get out of the situation. It may take several steps and some self-sacrifice, but it is possible to make change in your life. Let Zeus stand as a warning to ever giving in to such negative treatment. Remember, we are all virgin—that is, a woman complete unto herself, with no one "owning" her or having the right to use her.

REFERENCES

Bolen, Jean Shinoda. *Gods in Everyman: A New Psychology of Men's Lives and Loves.* New York: HarperPerennial, 1989.

Cunningham, Scott. *Magical Herbalism: The Secret Craft of the Wise.* St. Paul, Minn.: Llewellyn Publications, 1982.

Farrar, Janet, and Stewart Farrar. *The Witches' God.* Custer, Wash.: Phoenix Publishing Inc., 1989.

Goodrich, Norma Lorre. *Priestesses.* New York: HarperCollins Publishers, 1989.

Walker, Barbara G. *The Women's Encyclopedia of Myths and Secrets.* New York: HarperCollins Publishers, 1983.

Webster's New Twentieth Century Dictionary, Unabridged. New York: Simon and Schuster, 1983.

Interior design by Karin Simoneau
Typeset in Centaur and Bickham Script
Printed on Miami HiBulk White paper
by Friesens